WILD ABOUT Teddington & Bushy Park

THE RIVER, THE PARK AND THE HEARTBEAT OF A VILLAGE

By Andrew Wilson

With history consultant Ken Howe

In support of

Kindly sponsored by

For Josie, my springer spaniel, who has been on this book journey with me since the beginning in 2009 and is now over 16 and sadly, very unlikely to make it through to my next volume.

Introduction

Welcome to the 25th edition in my series of London Village Books. As followers of my work will know, I am at heart a nature photographer, and ensure that this forms the backbone of all that I do. So, wherever I stroll around London, I am always on the hunt for green open spaces. However, Teddington was easy, as right on its border is one of London's finest Royal Parks, Bushy Park, which I actually prefer to the one in Richmond (but please don't tell them I said that). So, what better way to celebrate this wonderful part of town than combining a look at the town itself and its wonderful park.

As is normal, all this magic doesn't just happen and there are many people I have met along the way, who have helped me produce this latest volume. There are far too many to mention you all by name but you know who you are and thank you. However, I should like to highlight a couple of people, as without them this current book could never have come about. First and foremost, Lisa Wyborn, who I met through the local organisation she helped run, Teddington Together (she left in the summer, as she came to the end of her tenure) and she helped introduce me to many local residents and essentially got me started. She is a hugely positive person and anyone who knows her can never quite understand where she finds all the time that she does to help people (on top of a full-time job). Lisa introduced me to Ken Howe, who is the local history supremo, who kindly provided me with an introduction and many extra facts on the some of the people and places that we have included in the book. Lisa was the conduit to the other members of her organisation and they helped shape the book's town content. One of the many initiatives we came up with, was helping to promote shopping locally and Teddington Retail Heroes was born. We nominated 20 of our finest independent retailers and through the summer I met them all and took their pictures. We hope you like what we have done and do please support all our local shops, as they are all heroes and where would we be without them.

Besides the many lovely people I met, I would also like to thank my sponsors, whose help financially is of course key. My books take over a year to produce and this valuable source of revenue is a lifeline for me. Lastly, there is my other historian, Caroline MacMillan, who has worked on many of my recent books and kindly helps out with any extra text I need and also proof reading. Caroline is great and I look forward to working with her on our next project..

Thank you again for supporting my work; I love this area and I hope that a little of this passion leaps off the pages as you glance at my latest photography.

Andrew Wilson
October 2022

Below: My lovely springer spaniel, Josie, down by Teddington Lock

Contents

Introduction	2	Stanley Road	66
A Short History of Teddington	4	Waldegrave Road	70
A Walk in Teddington	10	Church Road	72
Teddington Lock & Weir	**12**	Park Road & the Station	74
Autumn	14	Teddington Station	77
Winter	21	Ferry Road & Broom Road	78
Spring	25	Kingston Lane	85
Summer	33	Teddington at Christmas	88
Street Life	**38**	**Bushy Park**	**90**
The Queen's Jubilee Long Weekend	40	Winter	98
High Street	48	Spring	136
Teddington Lawn Tennis Club	58	Summer	152
Broad Street	60	Autumn	180

A Short History of Teddington

by Ken Howe, local resident and eminent local historian

Teddington was a sleepy village alongside the River Thames. Question. How old is the town? – Answer. We don't know.

A high class Bronze Age burial took place in Sandy Lane which has been dated to around 1500 BC, but it is unlikely that this was placed in the middle of the settlement which existed at that time. A huge number of weapons and other artefacts have been recovered from the River Thames at Teddington Lock and these cover a vast age range but there is no sign of an early settlement in the Bronze Age. Julius Caesar is said to have crossed the Thames along our stretch of river and given battle with the local Britons but Brentford, Kingston and Sunbury, to name but three, all claim this same distinction. However Romano-British dwellings have been discovered at Lower Teddington Road and Udney Park Playing Fields.

What we do know is that there was a small Saxon settlement here at the time of the Norman Conquest and the town takes its name from its Saxon spelling – Tudincgatun (the town of Tuda's people); the earliest documentation was in 968 AD.

Teddington formed part of the Saxon kingdom of Mercia and prior to the Conquest was ruled by Earl Leofric and his wife, Lady Godgifu, better known by her popular name of Lady Godiva. They were loyal subjects of King Edward the Confessor and when Edward sought to build a new abbey at Thorny Island (now Westminster), they were quick to support him and donated the Manor of Teddington to serve the new abbey.

The Norman Conquest made little difference to the village as it was already under the control of the Abbot of Westminster and the Normans did not mount any interference. The population was about 200, all working on the land

Opposite - Now and Then: The Weir as it was in the 1940's, with very low trees and as it is today.

Top - Now and Then: Looking west towards Broad Street in the days of the tram and as it today.

Above: The lock and weir as it is today. Thank you to Angela and Carol Ann from the marketing department of the new Teddington Riverside for allowing access to one of their penthouses to take this picture.

and each quarter a monk from the abbey would visit to check on the crops and collect the tithes.

The Plantagenets did not bring about any changes as the Wars of the Roses were too far away to make any impression. With the advent of the Tudor dynasty, Cardinal Wolsey acquired nearby Hampton Court and set about transforming it into a magnificent palace. This must have provided employment for many local craftsmen which probably increased when Henry seized the palace from Wolsey.

Henry VIII decided to extend his hunting grounds from Hampton Court and needed Teddington to complete the Great Chase in the Honour of Hampton. Negotiations were entered into with the Abbot of Westminster and Teddington was exchanged for Hurley Priory in 1536. Henry let out the Manor, apart from the hunting rights, and for the first time in 500 years, Teddington had a live-in Lord of the Manor.

Henry died in 1547, and was succeed by Edward VI followed by Mary Tudor and then Elizabeth I.

We know that Elizabeth was fond of this area and the Royal Court papers contain a letter written to her in 1570 by Robert Dudley, Earl of Leicester, written from Queen Elizabeth's Hunting Box, a hunting lodge in what is now Teddington High Street.

A succession of tenants took leases on the Manor from 1545 until the last one died in 1860. In 1801 the population had increased to 699 people living in 118 houses but by 1861 1,183 people occupied 215 houses. The executors put the Manor up for sale in 1861 but not as a single unit, instead the manor lands which covered about half of the area of Teddington, were broken

Now and Then: Peg Woffington's Cottages - a small terrace of 18th century, two-storey double-fronted cottages, with a plaque dated 1759. Peg Woffington was a popular Irish actress who lived in Teddington and died in 1760. She was buried in St Mary's Church. The cottages now enjoy Grade II Listed status. Local legend proclaims that Peg Woffington gifted the cottages to the poor of Teddington but nothing has ever been found to confirm this.

Top Right: The lock as it was originally, from a painting hanging on the wall in the lock-keepers office.

down into individual building plots.

The London and South Western Railway was making its way to Teddington and 1st July 1863 saw the opening of Teddington Station with the line running from Waterloo via Richmond and Twickenham to Hampton Wick.

Kingston had missed out on an earlier opportunity to connect with the railway, which had gone to Surbiton but made sure that this did not happen again. A bridge was built over the Thames and an extension to the track was made from Hampton Wick to Kingston, completing the loop line to and from Waterloo.

With the increase in new buildings, the area saw a rapid growth in local population increasing from 4,063 in 1871 to 6,599 in 1881 and 10,052 by 1891 and the small village had been transformed into a town. Still more building continued with about 1,000 new houses being built in each decade from 1891 to 1911.

There was no industry in Teddington as it had always been an agricultural village, the only exception being a wax candle factory in Waldegrave Road and a small boat building operation at the riverside. Now a variety of shops of every kind grew up along the Broad Street and the High Street and in 1902 a new employer came to town in the shape of the National Physical Laboratory (NPL) which still remains the town's greatest employer. The NPL was to play a large part in the Second World War; their huge water tanks were used in the development of the bouncing bomb by Barnes Wallis, the invention of degaussing machines to demagnetise our shipping from magnetic mines, the Mulberry floating harbours used on D-Day and PLUTO – the PipeLine Under The Ocean. Today it leads the world in the study of measurement and standards.

In 1912 a group of enthusiastic amateur film makers started using the facilities of Weir House to make five minute silent 'quickies'. Production increased and the house and its grounds were taken over by Master Films in 1918 to produce full length feature films. More changes took place and in 1931 Warner Brothers took a lease on the studios to make low budget "quota quickies" to satisfy British legislation and many household names served their apprenticeship here, it was said that 10% of all British films were made in Teddington. However, an enemy V1 flying bomb put an end to that on 5th July 1944, killing three people.

The studios reopened in 1948 but closed down again in 1952 and Warner Bros sold the studios to ABC Television. In 1967 ABC merged with Rediffusion to form Thames Television, probably the most successful independent television production company ever formed. They continued to operate until 31st December 1992 with a variety of sit-coms, drama, comedy and documentaries but when their franchise was up for renewal, Thames lost out to Carlton in a silent auction backed by the government. Teddington never recovered from the closure of Thames and the studios were sold off for exclusive housing.

In 2021 Teddington was named in the Sunday Times as "The best place to live in London", and was praised for its businesses, transport links and green space. "It is a small town that has shone – big enough to have everything you need within walking distance and small enough for everyone to feel connected."

Ken Howe
September 2022

Now and Then (Below): The view of Broad Street during a flood in the early 1900's and as it is today.

About Our Historian

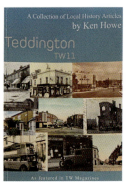

Ken Howe is a born and bred Teddingtonian, apart from the first two days spent in Chiswick Maternity Hospital. He became interested in history at an early age – "I had a very good history master at school" – and this developed into a study of the local history of his area and the stories of some of its residents. After a career in the insurance business, he was able to devote more time to local history. He is a past convenor of the History Group of the Teddington Society and a past chairman of the Borough of History Local History Society. He gained a Masters degree in History from Kingston University.

He has written extensively on Teddington history and his most recent publication is "Teddington TW11", a collection of his articles for the monthly magazine TW11. He has been a regular speaker on Teddington history subjects and personalities. He still lives in Teddington, is married to his wife Teresa and lives with a scheming cat called Felix.

Our historian, Ken Howe, is connected with several local organisations.

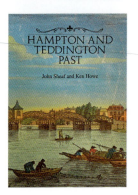

The Teddington Society was formed in 1973 as an amenity group to preserve and enhance the quality of life of everyone working and living in Teddington, largely through avoiding planning blight and supporting local causes and charities. There are several working groups within the Society, Corporate, Environment, Gardens, History, Planning. Riverside and Transport, each contributing to the continued wellbeing of Teddington.

The Borough of Twickenham Local History Society was formed in 1962 before the Borough was annexed by the Greater London Borough of Richmond Upon Thames, the Society was formed to cover the local history of Twickenham, Whitton, Teddington and the Hamptons.

Park Lane Stables

When she was threatened with eviction little did Natalie O'Rourke know that she would create her very own little bit of local history.

Natalie has a love for horses and wanted more than anything to run a stable but no ordinary stables, one that catered for children and adults with disabilities. Through sheer hard work, love and determination she achieved her goal and even found a way through COVID.

But just as she was hoping things might get back to normal, news came through that her landlord was selling up and unless she could find £1M, she would have to leave. Although a massive amount of money, somehow her fundraising caught the imagination of the population, both at home and across the country and she was able to raise the money.

Currently, working out of Ham, they hope to be back at their home in Park Lane soon. You can read Natalie's story in her very own book, Only Heroes & Horses.

Teddington Hospital

Having decided on building a new hospital as part of the War Memorial, the next step was to prepare an actual monument. The job was put out to tender and won by C M Moss, Monumental Mason of Church Road. Mr Moss was a local councillor and had also lost a nephew, Major Thomas Moss MC, in the conflict. He selected a four sided block of Portland stone, 18ft high at a cost of £76,000. On the north face there are 82 names from 1914/15, on the west face 52 names from 1916, on the east face 51 names from 1916 and on the south face 152 names. Subsequent enquiries have found that the original figure of 337 was wildly out and research has increased this number to in excess of 470.

As the dust of the Great War settled, the people of Teddington gave some thought as to how the fallen should be remembered. Wallace Elmsie, whose only son, Lieutenant Kenward Elmsie, had been killed in action, proposed that the town's most fitting memorial to its 337 dead would be a new hospital. This suggestion was endorsed by the Hospital Committee without dissent. The old six bed Teddington and Hampton Wick Cottage Hospital had already outgrown its efficiency before 1914 and a big change was needed. A massive fund raising campaign was started by the Committee Chairman, F Hugh Munby, who gave his every waking hour to the cause. On 19th March 1928, the foundation stone was laid by Lord Dawson of Penn, the King's Physician. Hugh Munby undertook a tour of the new Teddington and Hampton Wick Memorial Hospital, shortly before submitting to an early death. The Hospital has continued to survive and thrive throughout some turbulent times and some indifferent Ministers.

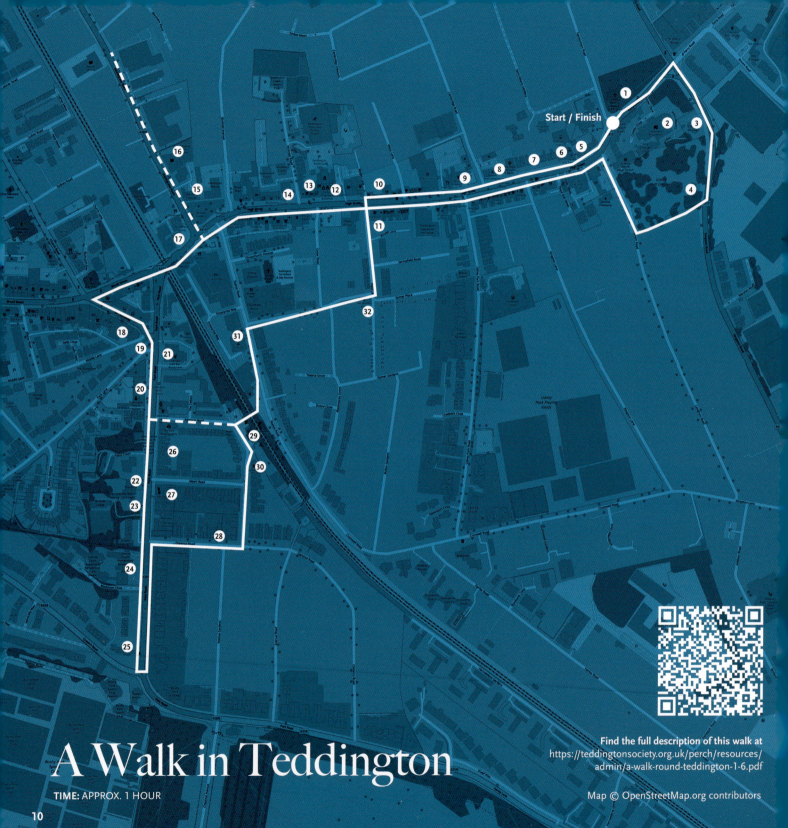

A Walk in Teddington

TIME: APPROX. 1 HOUR

Find the full description of this walk at
https://teddingtonsociety.org.uk/perch/resources/admin/a-walk-round-teddington-1-6.pdf

Map © OpenStreetMap.org contributors

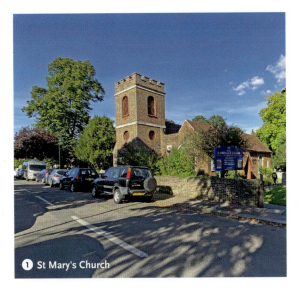
① St Mary's Church

④ Udney Hall Gardens

⑮ Elmfield House

㉜ Builders Arms

This is an edited version of a walk you can find on the Teddington Society's website (walk number 1, where you will find the full transcript and the map) and we are grateful to them for allowing us to share it with you. It takes you on a route covering many of the places featured in this book.

The parish church of St. Mary (1) was a chapel on the site in the 16th century whilst towering St. Alban the Martyr was built in 1896. But not every one liked the French Gothic style and as the number of worshippers diminished the Landmark Arts Centre (2) opened in 1995 and so the congregation returned to St Mary's. Turn right into Kingston Road and through Udney Hall Gardens (4), Udney House on the corner of Kingston Lane was the site of Sir Charles Duncombe's 17th century estate and said to be the richest man of the day.

Turn left into the High Street, Peg Woffington, a famous actress lived in one of the terraced houses in 1759 (5) and where she entertained the famous actor David Garrick. Next door is Oak Cottage (6), the oldest house in Teddington and dates back to Tudor times.

Further down the street, old buildings were pulled down in the 1860s and Harrow, Eton, and Oxford Villas (7) now stand there, next door is Cambridge House (8) now the Royal British Legion premises. The King's Head (9) dates back to 1689 and further along is Shambles Wine Bar (10), 'shambles' being the name for a slaughter house and parts of the building date back three centuries

The old vicarage on corner of Vicarage Road (13) was demolished in 1881 to make way for new housing, until the early 1900s cows were kept in fields behind the dairy. Reaching the junction of Waldegrave Road is Elmfield House (15) built around 1700 and just a few doors down Waldegrave Road is one of the 660 libraries (16) Andrew Carnegie, the Scottish-Philanthropist financed in the 1906.

Head up Broad Street and turn into The Causeway and between Middle Lane and Park Lane and admire two early 19th century houses, Adelaide and Clarence House (19). On the opposite side of the road was an ancient tavern, which by 1840 was The Clarence and finally became the Park Hotel (21). Bear right into Park Road where the residents of Teddington built the granite water fountain to commemorate the 1887 Jubilee for Queen Victoria, it was restored in 2002.

Local roads are reminders of the various descendent of Queen Victoria and at the corner of the Adelaide pub turn into Albert Road to reach the Railway pub (30). Teddington Station (29) opened in 1863 and received an arson attack by the suffragettes in April 1913. Walk over the bridge and along Station Road, where you will find an industrial estate where once stood the former Coal Office. The Teddington Cheese Shop (31), has been there for more than 20 years and a little further down Christ Church is now being converted into apartments. Turn right into Bridgeman Road, RD. Blackmore the author of Lorna Doone lived in Gomer House where Doone Close is today. Left at the Builders Arms (32), sadly, another of our lost pubs and so into Field Road, which leads you back to the High Street where the walk ends at the parish church of St. Mary.

11

Teddington Lock & Weir

There are in fact three locks that make up Teddington Lock, together with the weir. Built in 1810, and rebuilt in 1857, the weir and locks mark the tidal limit on the Thames.

Before the residential developments took place alongside the river, boat building was a feature for the area and where The Wharf restaurant now stands was once the site of Tough Bros Boatbuilders, see below, top left. The firm was founded by Douglas and Gordon Tough in 1917. They acquired the premises of Porter & Brice and Tom Bunn's Boatyard in 1928 to use as a repair/maintenance yard for their pleasure boats operating at Battersea. The yard gradually changed to building their own boats and when WWII came, they were well sited for the construction of motor torpedo boats and motor gun boats. This saw an increase in staff numbers from 16 to 220 and 44 boats in the "Fairmile" series were completed. From this yard Douglas Tough was famously commissioned by the Admiralty to commandeer all small boats on the Thames to take part in the Dunkirk evacuation. Over time, the viability of boat building in UK diminished and sadly the yard closed in 1973 and the area was redeveloped into luxury accommodation.

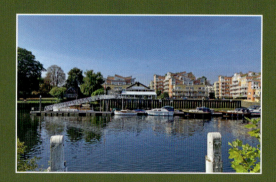

Autumn

November is traditionally the time of year when the downstream part of the river is allowed to find its own level, thus allowing any maintenance to be conducted at low tide. This is arranged by the barrier at Richmond Lock not being raised, which normally keeps the water level between the lock and Teddington artificially high at low tides.

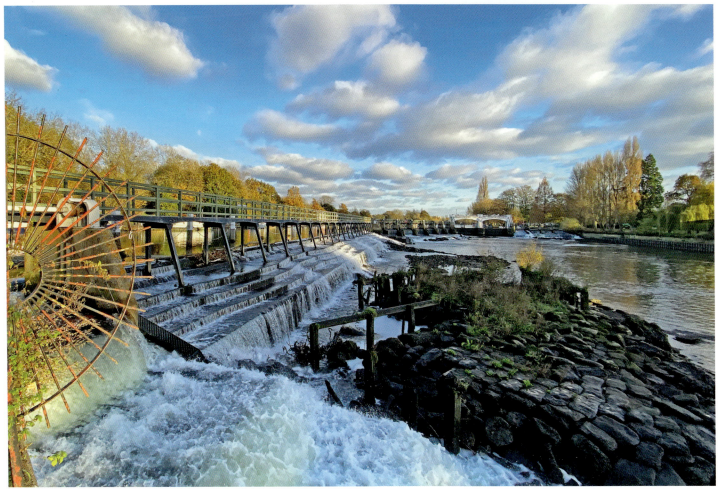

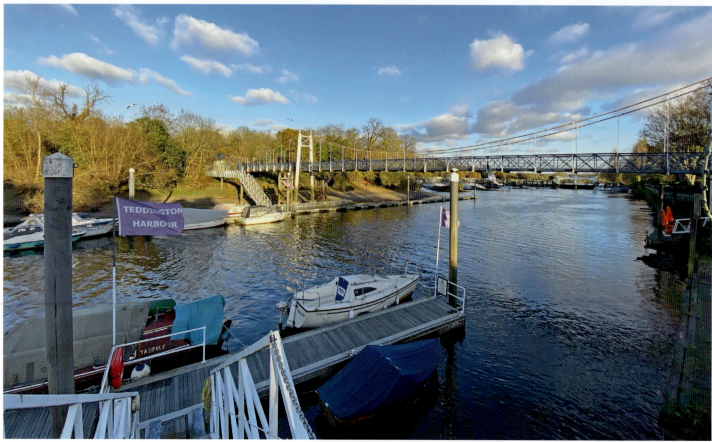

Winter

The first lock was built in 1811, it was unpopular with local fishermen and bargemen who cut the locks and the lock keeper had to keep them at bay with his blunderbuss in order to ward off attacks. It collapsed under the cumulation of weight of ice in 1829 but was eventually restored in 1871.

Spring

After thawing snow and the return of flowers, spring means we're finally able to enjoy time outside again.

Teddington Obelisk

Standing amongst trees and foliage the Teddington obelisk looks pretty neglected. The Obelisk marks the boundary of the jurisdiction of the Port of London Authority and the Environment Agency.

The plaque was erected in 1909 and refurbished in 2016.

The Anglers Pub

The Anglers has existed since the mid 18th century. The place was popular among local fishermen, who would spend hours on the river bank. Acquired by Fuller's around 2010, it remains a vibrant riverside pub. With its beautiful riverside setting, you can even arrive at the pub by boat and moor up right alongside.

Nature's Anglers

Followers of my work will know I am very fond of great crested grebes. So I was pleased to spot this pair back in the spring. However, with so many places to choose from, I never did find where they found a spot to nest. So I was happy in August to discover that they had been successful and had reared three chicks, who were now several weeks old. It's interesting to note how the adults seem to instinctively know who is next to be fed and viciously chase away the others (middle right).

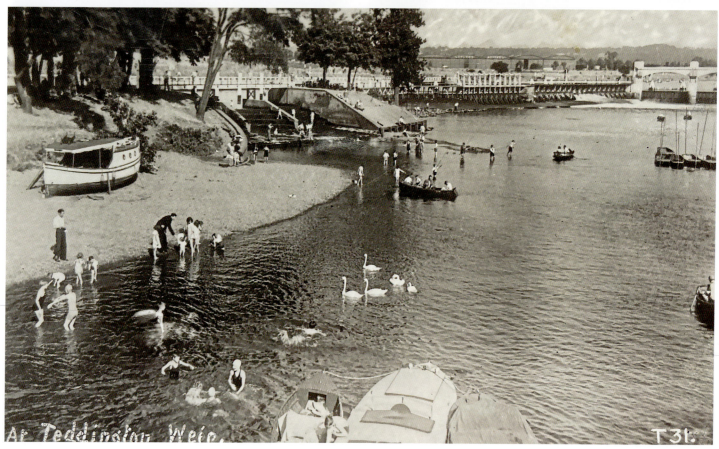

At Teddington Weir.

Summer

A popular spot for sun worshippers and bathers through the years, during Covid the locks were closed to the public and only reopened in the late summer of 2022.

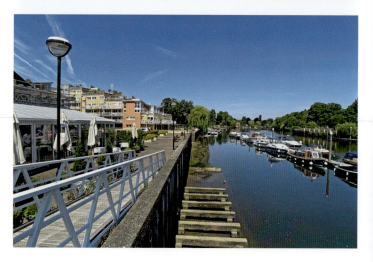

Clockwise from top left: Broom Road, Maddison Close, Clarence Road, Wades Lane and the High Street.

Spring comes to Teddington

I am not a fan of the cold, so I am always pleased to see the arrival of spring.

Clockwise from top left: Broom Road Recreation Ground, Clarence Road and the High Street.

Street Life

Prior to the coming of the railway, the main road ran through the village from the River Thames to the outskirts of Hounslow Heath on the western side. The railway line cut through almost the middle of the town and for two years whilst the railway construction was in progress, it was not possible to pass through this route. As a result the dissected main road developed in different ways. The High Street, which was the older part of the town, was still primarily the accommodation end with shops growing out of the front gardens of established houses. On the other side of the newly built bridge, the Broad Street concentrated on commercial retail buildings with room for accommodation above.

To this day, this has created a sense of elitism with the High Street occupants feeling superior to the Broad Street, for no good reason other than the age of foundation.

Above: The high street looking west, in the days of the tram.

1926-2022

The Queen's Jubilee Long Weekend

We all love a good excuse for a street party and the Queen's Jubilee in 2022 was no exception. Over the course of 4 days at the beginning of June, I visited no less than 16 street parties in Teddington and great fun they all were. A huge thanks to those that offered me a glass of the finer stuff and the odd cake. My pictures of the Queen (here and on the last page) were taken by me when she visited Richmond Park on the occasion of her last Jubilee in 2012.

Clockwise from middle left: Blackmores Grove, Broom Water West and Blandford Road.

Clockwise from top left: Clonmel Road, Clifton Road, Connaught Road and Clifton Road.

This page: the top four pictures: Fulwell Road.

Far left: Fulwell Road and the other three pictures from Langham Road.

Opposite page: the top two pictures from Manor Road and the other five from Munster Road.

43

Top three pictures: Railway Road (and love the shop sign).

Middle left: Rosebank Close

The other pictures: The special party put on in Udney Hall Gardens by the local Rotary Society and supported by the RNLI.

Top two pictures: Udney Hall Gardens
The other four: Victor Road (loved the cakes).

Top left: Watt's Lane and the rest from Wick Road, who invited a fabulous George Michael tribute act and I love the painted house, a true expression of how to go that extra mile.

Oopposite top right: Your author flanked by my good friends Cathy and Woody, who surpised me in Blackmores Grove, as I had forgotten where they lived.

1926-2022

High Street

Since February 1932, 135 High Street has been the home of Teddington Royal British Legion Club (below left). A social hub where Armed Forces and Public communities socialise in a wonderful setting, whilst striving to fulfil the values and charitable aims of the British Legion.

Now and Then: The high street as it was looking west and as it is today.

Opposite top right: After a magnificent display of ceramic poppies at the moat of the Tower of London in 2014, the Tower were selling off the actual poppies with all proceeds going to the Royal British Legion and five other charities. Elizabeth Foster acquired one of these and the Teddington Society had another. It was decided to mount a display for the following Remembrance Sunday in 2015 using the poppies as the central part of the backdrop. The Council agreed to the display being temporarily displayed outside Harlequin House with an inscribed copy of "In Flanders Fields" by John McCrae. This has proved very popular with the townsfolk of Teddington and has resulted in the display remaining in situ for the time being.

Teddington Retail Heroes

Shambles Restaurant & Wine Bar

Run by brother and sister, Massimo and Margarita, the name harks back to a time 250 years ago when the premises was a slaughter house. Popular with locals, and preferring to use quality seasonal produce, they have a beautiful garden area for alfresco dining, with their own kitchen garden on the side.

Teddington Retail Heroes

The Fallow Deer

Set up in 2013 by Alex, this cafe and bar is open seven days a week. Specialising in great seasonal produce, with everything cooked on site, they are known for their big breakfasts, brunches and lunches.

Above left: Nils, Mr Teddington Window Cleaner.

Above middle: Teddington Arms. If you had visited the High Street during the 1960 and 1970s, you would have found The Tooting Tyre Co premises at numbers 38-40, which had traded successfully for many years. Through the 80s and 90s it became a wine bar and Italian restaurant and in 2002 it was purchased by an independent pub chain and renamed "The Teddington Arms". Later taken over by the Green King brewery, it is still trading successfully, having become the predominant sporting pub in the town.

Teddington Retail Heroes

Elements

Gracing the high street since 2001 and run and owned by Clare, she and her team have won many awards. Proudly independent, they are very active, supporting many of the local schools and organisations.

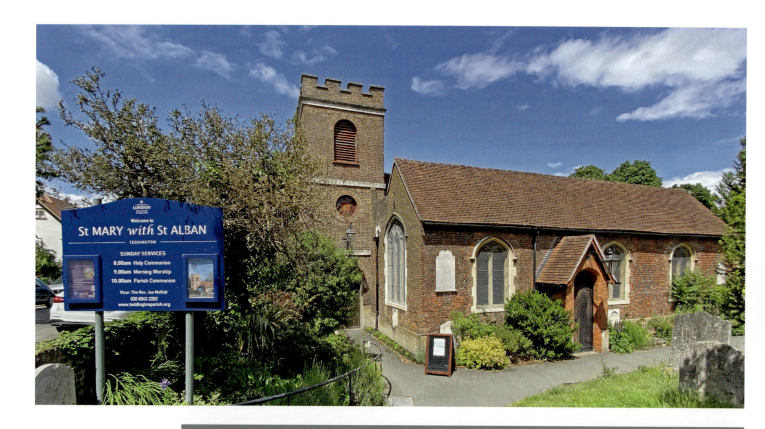

Above: There is evidence of the first chapel in Teddington in 1217. The next major development did not take place until the early 16th century when the South aisle was built. From here the parish church of St Mary evolved. When the size of the church became inadequate and on the building of the new church of St Alban, St Mary's closed in 1889. Fortunately St Mary's was never demolished and with a diminishing congregation, St Alban's was deconsecrated in 1977 and St Mary's was reopened as the parish church again under the revised name of St Mary with St Alban.

Teddington Retail Heroes

Gillian Million

This bridal emporium opened in 2009. Gillian and her team of fine artisans take a very hands-on approach to helping all their brides have the very best wedding day ever.

Teddington Retail Heroes

One One Four

Run by husband and wife team, Sam and Alex, they try to be a little different, mixing innovation and international cuisine with an openness and rootsy warmth - contemporary dining in a relaxed environment.

Below: This magnificent building was the product of the ambition of the Teddington parish priest, the Rev Francis Leith Boyd, and opened in 1889. As we have documented, with a diminishing congregation, it closed in 1975. It then suffered from years of neglect and vandalism until under the threat of demolition, a vigorous local campaign saved the church and in 1995 it reopened as the Landmark Arts Centre. Playing host to a variety of arts related events, the Landmark has made a solid contribution to community life in the town.

Teddington Retail Heroes

Refill Larder

For those looking to live a more sustainable life, this is the store for you. Opened by Kate in 2019, you'll find a myriad of household goods and foods to restock your home.

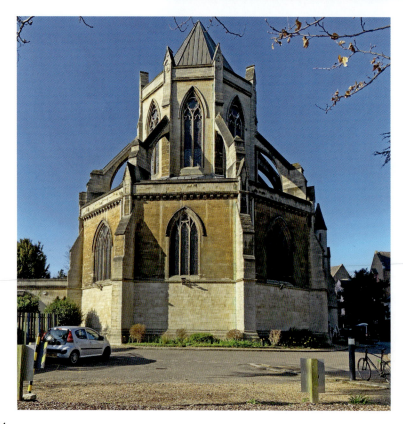

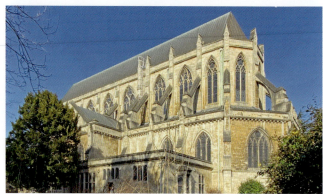

Teddington Retail Heroes

One Hundred High Street

100 Styles, 100 Looks, 100 Different Body Shapes.

A small independent boutique run by Sue and Debbie, dedicated to dressing and styling women of all ages. Sourcing an eclectic mix of wearable labels, they also offer a jeans fitting service.

Savills arrived on the high street in April 2022 and why did it take them so long you might say. They are here now though and Rory (below second right, pictured on their opening day) and his team bring a wealth of local knowledge and the power of one of this country's leading estate agents. I was pleased to see local director, Robin, helping to keep the place tidy.

Above left: The High Street has long been considered the oldest part of Teddington and it should not be surprising that some of the oldest pubs originate here. The original King's Arms was a beer house which consisted of three separate cottages occupied by Samuel Cole in 1851. In 2008 it changed its name to The Clockhouse, however this wasn't successful and was saved in 2020 and returned to its original name.

Opposite top: The King's Head is the oldest pub in Teddington still trading.

It was almost certainly in existence when we find our first reference which was 1689 for the Court Leet to be held at The King's Head. The Court Leet was the forerunner to the parish vestry or parish council, but acting solely for the Lord of the Manor. It closed in 2010 and was completely refurbished by French celebrity chef, Raymond Blanc.

Teddington Lawn Tennis Club

Teddington Lawn Tennis Club was founded in 1908 by the Teddington Baptist Church Sunday School. Known then as the Queens Road Tennis Club, it moved to its present site in Vicarage Road in 1914, changing its name in the process. Middlesex County Club of the Year in 2019, the club is a popular local haunt with all the back up, skills and fun you would expect from a thriving modern tennis club.

Broad Street

Now and Then: Broad Street as it was looking east and as it is today.

Teddington Retail Heroes

Teddington Carpet Centre

A family business, Teddington Carpet Centre has been a feature of Broad Street for over 50 years, and is Teddington's 2nd oldest business. The original family shop was Garrud's.

Now run by Rob, the son of the original founder and Sharon, his office manager believe the source of their success is down to treating each job as if it was their own home or business. They celebrated their 60th anniversary in 2022.

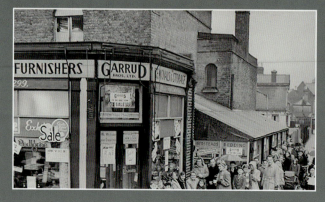

Teddington Retail Heroes

Mimmo

Teddington's oldest Cafe, Mimmo opened in 1997 and has been run by the same family for 23 years. Very popular with locals, Hani, one of the owners is pictured at his richly decorated pizza oven.

One of Britain's finest runners, Mo Farah, and a local resident was honoured with his own gold postbox, which lies just off Broad Street in North Lane.

Now and then: The Causeway as it was and as it is today.

Teddington Retail Heroes

Teddington Photographic

Steve Heybourne, who has run Teddington Photographic for the last 15 years, has been into cameras ever since his days at art school. A really excellent camera shop is a rare thing these days, so Teddington is lucky to have this shop. An authorised dealer for a range of household names, they are perhaps better known for second hand cameras, which they buy and sell.

Teddington Retail Heroes

The Loft

It is rare to find a high street these days with both a decent book store and a gift shop. So I am a big fan of this store and Cher (on the right, with her colleagues Debbie and Jenni) runs the store with her husband. A Teddington fixture for the last 19 years, The Loft is much more than just a gift store and offers a full range of things for the home, as well as running an excellent online store.

Top left: Albert Sims opened a jewellers shop in The Causeway in 1902 and the business has flourished ever since. His son joined him and in the course of time, the trade changed to opticians. Grandson Graham also came into the shop which is now owned and managed by the 4th generation – Melissa, making it the oldest business still trading in Teddington.

Teddington Retail Heroes

Teddington Sports

When injury cruelly cut short his sports career, David Fudge, who has run Tedddington Sports since 2013, felt compelled to fill what he saw as a gaping hole locally for sports knowledge. A self confessed cricket nut, David went to Teddington School and sees it as his job in life to ensure that kids and adults alike, use equipment that is the right size, weight and quality for the level of competition they play.

Above: The Hogarth can trace its history back to the mid 1800's but only became The Hogarth in the 1960's. Run in its present form since 2016 by a couple of hospitality veterans, you might be surprised by its depth and that it has a beer garden at the back.

Above: Described as a backstreet community pub, this business has had a remarkable turnaround. Run down and unloved at the turn of the century, it was taken over by Rae Williams, one step ahead of being turned into a private house. The Mason's is the place to go to for a glass of real ale. No tv, no gaming machines, no food except rolls and crisps, and a juke box from yesterday.

Teddington Retail Heroes

Happy Potter

Run by owner, Una, and her manager Hannah, the Happy Potter has been hosting parties and workshops and spreading joy with pottery paints and pom poms for over 11 years! My daughter, who has helped me with my books on the odd occasion, can vouch for the therapeutic value of creating your own things and just walking through the door you can tell how much they enjoy what they do.

Stanley Road

In 1800, the year of the Enclosure Act of Teddington, what is now Stanley Road was merely a lane connecting Teddington to Twickenham. By 1862 it was known as Webb's Lane after the name of the farmer of the Manor Farm and consisted mainly of Maud Cottage, Manor Farm and its outbuildings and a few small dwellings near the junction with Shacklegate Lane.

Coversure was established in 1986 with a view to providing a high quality, good value insurance service to local people across the country through independently franchised broking businesses. Since then Coversure has grown rapidly and now boasts over 90 offices throughout the UK. Teddington is no exception and can help either private clients or local businesses. Behind their building in Stanley Road can be found Teddington Constitutional Club, which is a private social club.

Teddington Retail Heroes

Immortal Botanica

Cassandra, pictured below on the left with her colleague Geri, is a stylist and floral artist and founder of Immortal Botanica. She has been obsessively researching the world of artificial florals and designing professionally with longer lasting botanics for nearly 5 years. Cassandra has a huge personality, which fits perfectly with some of her amazing floral artworks.

Below: The Red Lion can trace its history all the way back to 1869. Its local people were most probably not born in Teddington and the pub helped to embed them in the town.

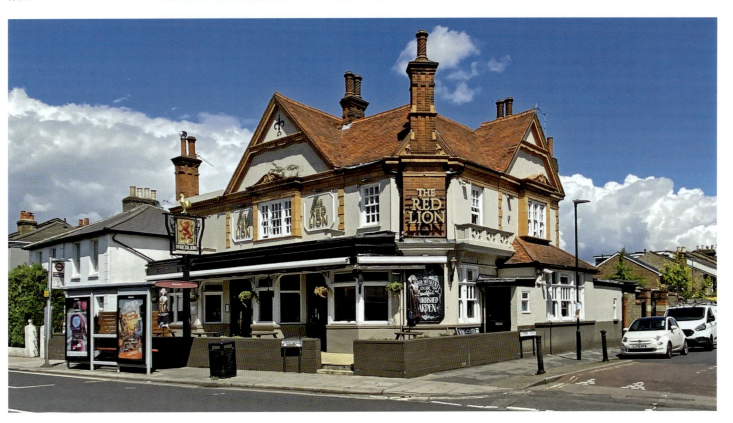

Teddington Retail Heroes

Perfect Pooch

Perfect Pooch Grooming was opened in 2009 by Ellie, seen here with her daughter, and takes pride in maintaining good relations with their local clients both the two legged & four-legged kind. As if to prove this, Ellie also runs a few doors down, Perfect You, so you can drop off your pooch and whilst you wait, get your own beauty treatment done.

Top Left and Middle, and Opposite: Stanley Road as it was and as it is today

Teddington Retail Heroes

Tiles of Wisdom

The Wisdom family, here represented by Stuart, a member of the current generation, has a long history in tiling reaching back almost 150 years. They provide a vast range of tiles from across Europe and a service that has been passed down through five generations.

Waldegrave Road

Waldegrave Road is one of the older roads in Teddington and besides housing the local library (opposite top), it also contains some fancy ironwork on some of the homes (below bottom). I was also fascinated to see that none other than Noel Coward was born here back in 1899. Sadly, The Waldegarve pub (right) looks to be another casualty of the COVID pandemic. Waldegarve Road also houses a modern office block, which in the right light can look rather impressive architecturally (below).

Above: We have Scots born American philanthropist Andrew Carnegie to thank for Teddington Library. He donated £3,350 towards the cost of the building which opened in 1906. Unlike some local libraries, it is open seven days a week, remaining open until 7pm a couple of nights a week.

Teddington Retail Heroes

Teddington Butchers
A family run business, Teddington Butchers can trace their history back 100 years. Besides all you would expect from a butcher, they specialise in free range and meat from a variety of rare breeds.

Church Road

The playground in Church Road is the site of the Willoughby Hotel (right) which was destroyed during the Blitz. The pub took a direct hit on the night of 29 November 1940 which happened to be the Loan Club pay-out night. Seventeen people were killed and the Willoughby was never re-built. The Abercorn Arms (bottom) was built in 1863, during the boom time for pubs and used to be part of Youngs. More recently, In 2016, it became member of the Big Smoke Brew Co family of pubs.

Teddington Retail Heroes

Roan Records

Roan Records began life in 1980 by Robert (right), who wanted to open a record store, and after forty years of uncareful planning and not even thinking about it, it has now appeared out of the mist and has settled in a corner of Teddington.

A couple moving into Teddington were looking to acquire premises that would be suitable for business as well as accommodation for them both. They purchased a house in Church Road and in the course of renovating the building, removed a layer of plaster on the outside to reveal the inscription of C M Moss – Monumental Mason.

At the end of the First World War, it was decided that the most respectful way to remember the war dead of Teddington would be to open a memorial hospital and this was duly done (see page 9). The job of providing a monument went out to tender and was won by C M Moss. He was also a local board councillor and had served on various Teddington committees. He had also lost a nephew in the war – Major Thomas Moss MC. The monument was a four sided block of Portland stone, 18 ft high on two steps at a cost of £76.00.

Teddington Retail Heroes

Vida

Vida, run by Louise Green, is a health and beauty spa and as one of her clients quotes, is a delightful and friendly oasis of calm in the centre of Teddington.

Teddington Retail Heroes

Sidra

Sidra is a very popular Lebanese restaurant, that has been catering to the local populous for over 20 years. Its a one-of-a-kind cafe experience where a wide range of freshly prepared and hand-made food is available.

Park Road & the Station

Below: Before becoming Teddington Cheese, their building was part of H Comfort & Sons, coal merchants.

Bottom left: The Adelaide Pub was built in 1863 and coincided with the arrival of the railway. Named after Queen Adelaide, the widow of William IV, who had returned to live in Bushy House after William's death. Very popular locally, she was the patron of the first local school and supported many local charities.

Bottom right: Surprisingly, The Railway was not built at the same time as when the railway line opened in Teddington in 1863 and it was not until 1867 that The Railway Refreshment Rooms came into being. After a succession of popular landlords took the pub to the end of the last century, after the millennium was celebrated, there was a change in the social attitude to pubs on a national scale. It closed its doors in 2006 and underwent a major refurbishment, reopening as a gastropub "The Bloated Mallard". A few years on and a change of ownership and the pub nearly regained its old name but merely became "The Railway".

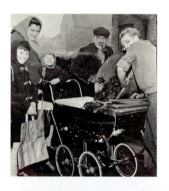

The Park Hotel can trace its history back to the early 1700's, when it was known as The Greyhound. As is normal with pubs, their names tend to reflect famous people of their times. The Park is no exception, with connections to Lord North (The North Arms) and The Duke of Clarence (The Clarence Hotel) in its lineage. It became The Park and Teddington's premier hotel as recently as 2000.

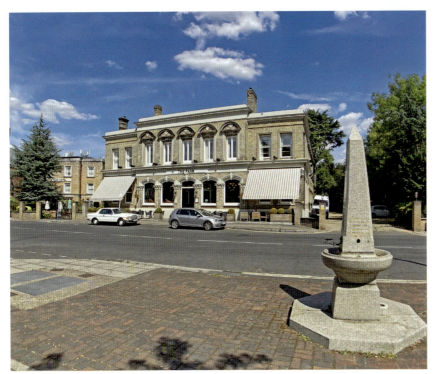

Left: Installed as part of Queen Victoria's Jubilee, the drinking fountain on the right, used to bear an inscription stating "Presented by 600 inhabitants of Teddington as a memento of the Jubilee of 1887." The plaque noting this has been lost through time and a further inscription has been etched to say "Restored by the residents of Teddington as a memento of the Jubilee of 2002 and 2012." The monument came about as a result of a competition to present a lasting memorial to celebrate Queen Victoria's Jubilee. It did not find favour with R D Blackmore who thought it ostentatious and said that if that was the best entry, he would have hated to see the worst. The Teddington Society has plans to bring the fountain back to use.

Teddington Station

The Richmond Railway Bill received the royal ascent on 21st July 1845 and the London and South Western Railway line opened at Richmond Station a year later.

A similar proposal to put a railway link through to Kingston had been rejected by Kingston as they had very strong coaching interests that blocked any alternative form of transport. The route was subsequently passed to Surbiton, thereby putting Surbiton very firmly on the map.

It is hard to say when the notion of extending the railway to Teddington was put to the villagers but most of them were agricultural workers or working on the land and the prospect of the railway would have meant little to them. Whatever negotiations went on from 1855 to 1861, the go-ahead was given and a compulsory purchase was made of all the land that the railway line required. At least two years of heavy work followed with the village being literally cut in half as the railway track was laid and a road bridge built over it.

The grand opening day came on 1st July 1863 when not only Teddington Station but also Hampton Wick and Kingston Stations were opened. Surprisingly there is no reference to this memorable occasion in the local press of the day. The railway continues to thrive and Teddington celebrated the 150th anniversary of its station on 30th June 2013.

Below: The footbridge at the station was built by the London and South Western Railway in 1863 to appease R D Blackmore whose land had been dissected by the coming of the railway. He had been a fierce opponent of the railway especially to the compulsory purchase of his land to complete it. This did not satisfy Blackmore and he maintained a hostile relationship with the railway until his death.

Ferry Road & Broom Road

Above and Right: The Teddington Film Studios were created in 1912. In their time, they were owned and operated by Warner Bros. who created 144 films here. On 5 July 1944 the studios were hit by a VI flying bomb killing the head of production, "Doc" Max Solomon and two others. They recovered from wartime to switch from film to television production and became hugely successful until Thames TV failed in the renewal of its franchise in 1992. The studios continued for a few years but were then dismantled and the site levelled in 2016 and are now a block of luxury apartments, Teddington Riverside. The studios at one time were the largest local employer.

The Lensbury Hotel

Situated on the Middlesex bank of the River Thames at Teddington Lock, the Lensbury, as it is known, makes a striking impression on all those seeing it for the first time. It was established in 1920 as the Lensbury Social and Athletic Club and was a club for employees of Shell Petroleum. This continued for many years and the first class facilities available were the envy of almost every other sporting organisation. Shell appointed Sir Peter Yarranton as General Manager in 1978 and under his direction, Lensbury's status as an international class sporting venue was established.

The 1990s saw a change in direction with the club opening to non-employees of Shell and the Shell subsidies being gradually whittled away. The name "Lensbury" was coined from part of the names of Shell's two major London offices at St Helens Court, Bishopsgate and 16 Finsbury Circus; the "Lens" from "Helens" and the "bury" from "Finsbury." Popular with some of our national teams, including the England rugby team, the England Soccer Lionesses recently celebrated their world cup victory whilst staying at The Lensbury.

LENSBURY AND BRITANNIC HOUSE ASSOCIATED CLUBS, TEDDINGTON

Teddington School

Teddington Secondary School for boys opened in 1962 and by 1985 girls were admitted. The former school building was demolished and in 2011 the new architectural designed school opened.

Tamesis Sailing Club

Possibly the latest sailing club to be launched, the Tamesis Club was founded in 1885 as a spin off from Thames Sailing Club in Surbiton. At first, they used the premises of Alfred Burgoine at Hampton Wick and then in 1901, they moved to their present location and after several extensions and improvements, the current handsome clubhouse, with a kitchen and bar was established. A very popular racing club, Tamisis has produced many Olympic and international helmsmen.

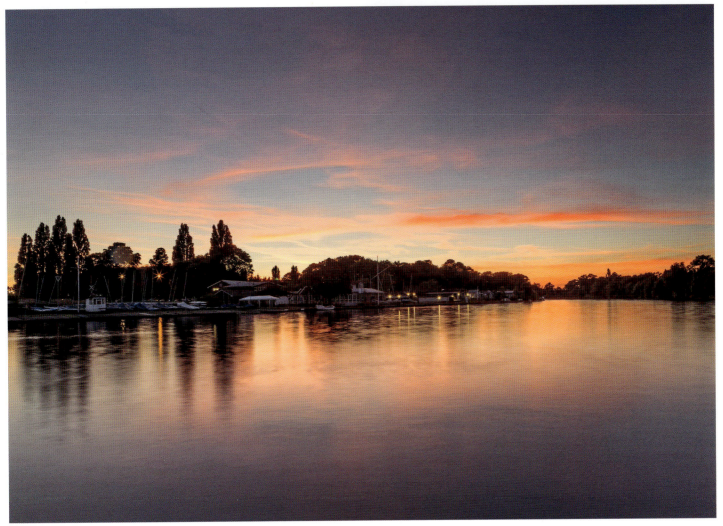

Left: The view of the Thames from the top of Thamespoint. Many thanks to my friend, Elaine, who lives in this block, for introducing me to an acquaintance of hers, who kindly let me in to take this picture from their terrace.

Kingston Lane

Left: Off Kingston Lane you can find the Udney Park Playing Fields, which were part of the estate of Robert Fullerton Udney, a successful West Indies merchant who died in 1802. In the early 1920s the fields were acquired by the Old Merchant Taylors as a War Memorial Ground to commemorate the Old boys lost in the Great War. The OMTs moved their club to a new location in 1937, leaving Teddington empty. More recently, the Playing Fields have been acquired by a property developer and they have that their plans somewhat thwarted by a covenant in place stating that the fields must be left for sport.

Above: Whilst investigating the Playing Fields, I was very taken with this front garden, number 57, and the owner kindly let me take these pictures.

Teddington Cemetery

The sleepy village of Teddington had seen some rapid growth in the 19th Century; firstly with the disposal of the manorial estate and the land being sold in single building plots and secondly with the coming of the railway in 1863. In 1801 the population of the village was 699 and this had increased to 1,183 in 1861, the year before the sale of the manor lands. By the turn of the century in 1901, it had grown to 14,038. For most of this time, there was only St Mary's Church to see to the spiritual needs of the villagers and only the single churchyard in which to bury them. After much deliberation and much infighting about how to find a suitable cemetery site or a way of extending the existing churchyard, it was decided that the Local Board would manage burials and the new cemetery was opened in 1879.

Teddington at Christmas

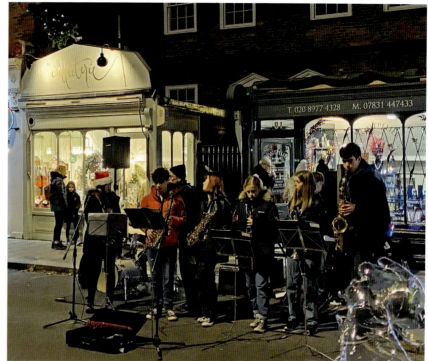

Bushy Park

At approximately 1,100 acres, Bushy is the second largest Royal park in London. It was once part of Hounslow Heath and after the Norman Conquest was owned and occupied by the Knights Hospitaller until acquired by Cardinal Wolsey who built a magnificent palace, Hampton Court, within the park. When he saw what Wolsey had built, Henry VIII was overcome with jealousy and seized the palace for himself.

Henry had grand designs on the estate and wished to create a Chase in the surrounding countryside and divided the park into three separate areas, Upper Park, Middle Park and The Wilderness, stocking them with deer and game. As part of his improvements he had the entire park enclosed in a brick wall, some of which still exists (picture maybe?).

Hampton Court has always been the home of royalty and Bushy Park has been considered as its garden.

Since Henry, there has been a succession of kings and queens although none of them have made the palace their permanent home. Originally the park stood in the parish of Hampton and over the years it has shifted into Teddington.

Charles I decided to create the Longford River by diverting eleven miles of the River Colne into Hampton Court to power the ornamental fountains.

For a brief spell, the royal connection was broken as Oliver Cromwell decided on Hampton Court and Bushy Park as his "royal" residence. The Restoration followed and the Groom of the Bedchamber, Edward Proger, became Ranger of the three parks and built a lodge in Middle Park and also the first Bushy House. He held the position for 48 years until his death at age 96. James II showed no particular liking for Bushy but William and Mary were reminded of Holland by the very flatness of the park.

Above left: A party in the park to celebrate the King's Jubilee in 1935.

Above: Chestnut Avenue around 1910 and the early days of the motor car.

The office of Ranger of Bushy Park was a popular one and much sought after by the gentry. The Earl of Halifax was one, Lady Ann North, wife of the Prime Minister who lost the American colonies another, William IV when Duke of Clarence and Queen Adelaide when William died.

At the outbreak of World War I, a large camp was constructed in Upper Lodge for Canadian troops and a hospital was made from buildings at Upper Lodge which became King's Canadian Hospital. When America entered the Second World War in 1942, they opened Camp Griffiss in Bushy Park. It was popularly held that this was due to an navigational error on behalf of the American army who were looking for Bushy Heath, Hertfordshire. The camp was headquarters of the U.S Eighth Army Air Force until October 1944 when it was taken over

by General Dwight Eisenhower as HQ to SHAEF – Supreme Headquarters of the Allied Expeditionary Force with Eisenhower as its overall commander. From here the invasion of Italy was planned and later, the D-Day landings.

The park has been used as a training ground by many different athletes – Sonia O'Sullivan from Ireland, the Kenyan middle distance team and our own four times gold medallist Mo Farrah. At the 2012 Olympics, Bushy Park was used as the finishing point for some of the distance cycling events and Bradley Wiggins gained one of his gold medals here. Nowadays the main use of Bushy is recreational with over 1,000 runners turning up every weekend for the "Bushy Fun Run."

Ken Howe
May 2022

For more pictures of the park please follow **@BushyParkPhotography** on Instagram.

Trees

There are many magnificent trees within the park and they are best seen in winter, when their leaves do not obscure their magnificent outlines. According to The Friends of Bushy & Home Park, there are 140 veteran trees of varying types, with the oldest being a Sweet Chestnut. Over 40 trees were lost or damaged during Storm Eunice in February 2022, including this Horse Chestnut (left) but thankfully none of the veterans.

Bushy House

The original Bushy House dates from 1663 and through various manifestations, it became a Royal residence in 1797 when the Duke of Clarence moved in. Queen Victoria offered it to the exiled King of France in 1865, who held onto it until his death in 1896. With no children to pass it onto, the house fell empty until it became part of the newly formed National Physical Laboratory (right) in 1902, which it remains part of to this day.

Winter

Winter, a lingering season, is a time to gather golden moments, embark upon a sentimental journey, and enjoy every idle hour.

JOHN BOSWELL

Diana Fountain

Designed in 1637 by Hubert Le Sueur at the request of King Charles I for his wife Henrietta Maria, this bronze statue of a goddess is set on a marble and stone fountain, surrounded by bronzes of four boys, four water nymphs and four shells.

Moved to its present site in 1713, the fountain was restored in 2009.

Deer

Bushy Park is a deer park where red and fallow deer still roam freely, just as they did when Henry VIII used to hunt there. There are around 320 deer and it is essential that their grazing continues in order to maintain the high wildlife of the park's grasslands. The herds are kept out of the Woodland Gardens and other plantations in order to protect the trees and shrubs.

Big Frosts

Bushy Park has its own micro climate and regular mists descend when the conditions are right. During the winter, you can witness some spectacular hoar frosts, which is when water vapour in the air comes into contact with the trees and plants that are below freezing.

Winter is the best time to see stonechats (far left and right) and to the photographers delight, they love nothing better than to stand proud on the tips of plants.

Swans

There are several pairs of swans in the park and their beauty hides a very aggressive side when they are staking out a territory or protecting their young. The numbers vary from year to year, with over 30 counted in the winter of 2021 but with nothing like that number in 2022.

The Park in the Snow

As with much of London, snow isn't that common with the last notable occurrence being the 'beast from the east' in 2018. During the production of this book, I only witnessed the odd dusting.

The Woodland Gardens

Behind the fence in the picture bottom left can be found the magical world of the Woodland Gardens. The look of the gardens took early shape when in 1925 two plantations were combined. The gardens were further developed in 1948 when the then Park Superintendent, Joseph Fisher, set about planning out the paths and much of the planting that you see today.

The gardens are also home to the Pheasantry Cafe, an essential stop for weary park goers and photographers alike.

Birds

The park is home to many birds, including the red crested pochard (opposite far left), little grebe (opposite top right), dancing black headed gulls (opposite bottom), little egrets (left) and cormorants (below).

Mistletoe

A striking feature amongst many of the trees in the park is the mistletoe. A parasitic plant, their presence doesn't kill their hosts but can over time weaken them. Birds are the unwitting disperser of mistletoe, which germinates directly on the bark of trees from the droppings left by the birds having gorged on their rather beautiful white berries.

The Blue Hour

The blue hour is a term that many photographers use to describe the lighting conditions pre-dawn and especially post-sunset.

During the winter, especially with a hard frost, the park can look very beautiful.

Spring

Spring is the time of year when it is summer in the sun and winter in the shade.

CHARLES DICKENS, GREAT EXPECTATIONS

Spring arrives to the sound of birds all over the park calling for a mate. The male swans forever fighting. The willows showing off their beautiful new colours. Coots foraging in herds and baby rabbits popping up amongst the grasses.

The Upper Lodge Water Gardens

Built as a private garden in 1710, this hidden gem within the park was restored in 1990's with help from the Friends of Bushy Park, finally reopening in 2010. It played a vital role last century during the two world wars, with the Upper Lodge (below bottom left) acting as a hospital during the first, and as a US barracks during the second. It has a resident pair of swans, who rather precariously, nest on the edge of the upper pond (below right). They were helped in the spring of 2022 by one of the park's rangers, Matt, with some straw for building their nest. Sadly, they were within a few days of hatching when a fox raided the nest.

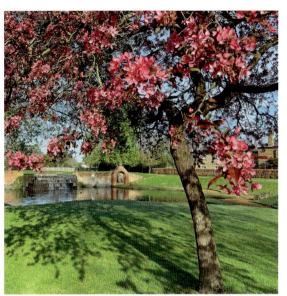

The Woodland Gardens

The gardens are a beautiful part of the park, especially with the arrival of the blossom, which can be as early as mid February. The gardens were designed with lots of colour and nature friendly plants in mind. With the returning warmth, visitors love nothing better than the chance to sit outside the Pheasantry Cafe.

Summer

In early June the world of leaf and blade and flowers explode, and every sunset is different.

JOHN STEINBECK

Now and Then: Feeding the deer is, of course, not allowed anymore but was clearly quite a thing 100 years ago.

The Longest Day

June 21st 2022 was rather a dull affair, or the end of the day was, and certainly no hint to the extraordinary weather that was to come. However, I was thrilled when a hind and her fawn appeared by Heron Pond and, standing perfectly still, the little thing looked straight at me.

Marbled white butterflies are one of my favourites and before the light totally faded, I was pleased to capture one amongst the pretty grasses.

The Water Gardens

Unlike the rest of the park, The Water Gardens are more manicured. In early June, it was fun to discover the grass covered in yellow hawkweed, which was a magnet for a meadow brown butterfly (bottom).

On this visit I also encountered a new family of mallard ducks. They were finding it hard to get out of the water as there is only one ramp in the lower pond and none in the upper pond. With the help of one of the park rangers, we eventually helped them out. Unfortunately, she then led them to the upper pond, where there is no escape bar going over the waterfall. Their journey took them past the rather impressive cave mural, that was kindly paid for by The Friends of Bushy Park (opposite bottom).

Butterflies

Wild flowers and nectar are a magnet for the butterflies in the park and I have never seen so many skippers (right and opposite). It wasn't until the second half of July that the gatekeepers arrived, which, to my mind seemed very late (bottom). With the butterflies, came the predators. They know where best to hide in amongst the flowers. For example, the grass spider below, who had caught a six spot burnet moth. Marbled white butterflies favour purple over most other coloured flowers, with thistle being a particular favourite (overleaf).

The Parkrun

It may now be a worldwide phenomenon, but Parkrun has its roots in Bushy Park. Back in October 2004, 13 runners and five volunteers took part in a time trial. The day I visited this summer, 16th July, was their 885th running of the event, and certainly now attracts far more people than 13.

The Long, Hot Summer of 2022

At the time of writing, this summer has been the driest since the famous summer of 1976. The park turned cream and gold, shade was at a premium and deer headed for the water.

Such a small wall was never going to keep the stags at bay, and besides the cooling water, this was one of the last remaining places where the plants were still lush.

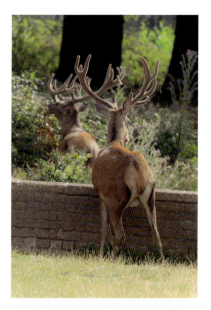

Birds in the Park

There are many kestrels in the park and it's fun watching the young ones taking their first steps into the world (opposite). The starlings like to congregate amongst the grasses to feast on the seeds and small invertebrates that they find there.

The Woodland Gardens

One of the attractions of the gardens, besides the welcome shade it offers and the Pheasantry Cafe, is the Longford River, that meanders through it. There is nothing like water to attract damselflies (opposite).

In June, there is a beautiful patch of Oxeye daisies, which this year attracted a mass of meadow brown butterflies (overleaf).

The Visitor Centre

The Friends of Bushy and Home Park helped fund a fabulous new visitor centre, which can be found next to the Pheasantry Cafe. It was opened by Andrew Scattergood, CEO of The Royal Parks, on 21st June 2019. Manned solely by volunteers, it is open at weekends and some week days.

For more information on this and the other good work that they do please visit fbhp.org.uk.

Fancy a picnic?

Don't be surprised if you are joined by some animal friends.

I am grateful to some of my photographic friends, who led me to this kestrel nest, which was conveniently near a path, offering great views. As they got near to fledging, the rangers cordoned off the area to protect them as they left the nest.

In the course of my travels, I am pleased to meet many people. No more so than, Lee Tilley (Instagram: @leetilleyphotography), who, besides being an excellent photographer, is also a fox rescuer with the Fox Angels Foundation.

He kindly introduced me to this little fox cub, who he was keeping an eye on throughout late spring and early summer. He was concerned that she was orphaned and wanted to ensure her wellbeing. We sat down in the grass and after a short time she came out and greeted us. What a thrill it was to be in the company of such a beautiful wild animal.

We were joined by my and everyone's favourite park photographer, Sue Lindenberg (@suelind7), who I have known for years.

Autumn

No Spring, nor Summer beauty hath such grace,
As I have seen in one Autumnal face.

JOHN DOONE

One of the distinctive features of the park, are its water features. They are all manmade and date back to Charles I. In 1637 he created the Longford River, as he wished to bring water to one of his residences, Hampton Court. During the 1650's this was extended to form the channels you see today and the picturesque Heron and Leg of Mutton Ponds.

The Rut

In September each year, the deer enter what is known as the Rutting season. The stags fight for the right to mate with the females, known as hinds. This involves a lot of noise, as the stags roar across the park.

Keeping their harems together and opponents at bay, can be an exhausting job, with most of the stags going without any food for up to six weeks. As with early summer and the birth of their young, everyone is asked to keep their distance during the rut, and for all dogs to be kept on a lead.

All rights reserved. No part of this publication may be reproduced, stored in any retrieval system or transmitted in any form or by any means, electronic, mechanical photocopying or otherwise without the prior permission of the copyright holders. Whilst every care has been taken in the production of this book, no responsibility can be accepted for any errors or omissions. The publishers have taken all reasonable care in compiling this work but cannot accept responsibility for the information derived from third parties, which has been reproduced in good faith.

First Edition – ©Unity Print and Publishing Limited 2022

History Consultant: Ken Howe

Designed by Kieran Metcalfe of Ascent Creative ascent-creative.co.uk

Proofreading: Caroline MacMillan
www.westlondonwalks.co.uk

Printed by Page Bros
www.pagebros.co.uk

Bound By Green Street Bindery
www.maltbysbookbinders.com

Colour Management by Paul Sherfield of The Missing Horse Consultancy
www.missinghorsecons.co.uk

Published by Unity Print and Publishing Limited, 18 Dungarvan Avenue, London SW15 5QU
Tel: +44 (0)20 8487 2199
aw@unity-publishing.co.uk
www.unity-publishing.co.uk

Most of the pictures in this book were taken using a Canon 6D plus lenses with some additional shots taken using an iPhone 11.

Follow Andrew on Twitter and Instagram
@WildLondonPics